To Gregor
Garost[...]

The teacher of Division
6 Grade 5 2003/2004
and my son Mujtaba
at Gordon Head
school with great
respect and many
thanks.

Best regards,
M. Huwaidj
_____
June 28, 2004

MOHAMMAD HUWAIDI

SAVED BY SIMPLE LOGIC

A CLASSICAL ANECDOTE

Robert D. Reed Publishers

Text ©2003 Mohammad Huwaidi
Illustrations ©2003 Ali Huwaidi

For information regarding permission, please write to:
Robert D. Reed Publishers
750 La Playa Street, Suite 647
San Francisco, CA 94121

ISBN 1-931741-18-2
Library of Congress Number: 2002102464
Printed in China

PREFACE

This story has been written specifically for young readers to think, analyse, and learn. Every phrase and word has been chosen carefully. Some new ideas have been introduced. New vocabulary has been presented. Parents and teachers need to encourage readers to learn these new words by looking them up in the dictionary and by practicing them.

Computers have evolved greatly and have invaded almost every house since their debut. The computer has become indispensable, being used daily by people of all ages and for all different purposes, including work, shopping, learning and amusement. Understanding binary logic is important if one is to understand digital computers. I personally think that kids should be exposed to logic as soon as they can understand it-in a simplified form, of course.

Readers are encouraged to read and analyse the story thoroughly before attempting to solve the exercises given at the end. Special attention needs to be paid to the subjective questions because they promote analysis and creativity.

I would like to thank my cousin, luminary-artist Ali Huwaidi, and acknowledge his permission to use his beautiful oil paintings in this story where the theme fits. Moreover, I would like to thank twin-sisters Reem and Aayyat for illustrating the story.

Finally, please send your constructive criticism and judgment to me by email at: Huwaidi@acm.org.

SEA-HAT

By the shore of an ancient sea is a town called Sea-Hat, so named because of the way it sits on the top of a lagoon shaped like a hat. Green, rolling farmland extends to the west; to the south, a lush forest flourishes; and to the north, a wall with few gates protects Sea-Hat against attack.

The people of Sea-Hat are generally hard working, simple, peace lovers who make their living in fishing, farming, and trading. Although most live hand-to-mouth[1], a few of the townspeople are wealthy and privileged.

3

THE HAARS

Hasse Haar is one of Sea-Hat's few wealthy townspeople. Among his many possessions are farms, palaces, and horses. He has only one son, whose name is Moe-Haar. Mead, Hasse's less wealthy older brother, also has a son, named Joe-Haar.

Hasse is a good person who helps the poor and the needy. One of those people whom he helps is Beebe, who lives in Hasse's palace. Beebe is the daughter of an old lady who used to live in the woods in a humble hut. Currently, Beebe is helping Hasse to raise his orphan son. She is good to people and to animals-indeed, she feels no threat from any animal. Most animals are sensitive to the purity of the person, and they know that Beebe is kind.

Hasse has always been a seeker of knowledge, tremendously fond of education. Therefore, he has employed one of the best pundits (i.e. Pascal) to teach Moe-Haar. Pascal has his own wing in the palace reserved for teaching, where he instructs not only Moe-Haar but also some other children, including Joe-Haar.

By nature, Moe-Haar loves to learn and explore. On the other hand, his cousin Joe-Haar does not, although

---

[1] I.e. is used in written English to mean namely.

both boys were given the same educational opportunities. Moe-Haar is good-natured, while Joe-Haar is not, and for this reason Pascal likes Moe-Haar. Moe-Haar is amicable and kind, while Joe-Haar is hostile and malicious; furthermore, Joe-Haar refuses to learn. The boys are ultimately as different as can be.

PASCAL TEACHING LOGIC

Pascal is a pundit, mathematician, astronomer, philosopher, and logician. Pascal is unique, and his knowledge is fundamental. Hasse appreciates Pascal's wisdom and intellect, and he is very keen to educate his son with the disciplines of Pascal. Further, Pascal uses his knowledge for the sake of good, not evil. Pascal truly understands that intelligence is a blessing that should never be abused.

Pascal possesses his own wing in Hasse's palace, complete with laboratories, classrooms, and an astronomical observatory, among other things. Pascal is treated with much respect, as he rightly deserves.

One of the many disciplines that Pascal has mastered and teaches is logic. Logic is sensible and simple. It is something that people practice every day, often without directly realizing it. They can prove their thoughts and arguments very easily when using logic.

At its abecedarian[2] form, logic is binary; i.e. a statement can only be true or false. The statements people make when they speak will either be true or false. Also, mathematical questions can be answered in either a true or false

---

[2]Basic and/or rudimentary. From now on, if you come across a new word, you need to consult either the selected dictionary at the end of the story, or refer to a reputable dictionary for better understanding.

manner. To know more about logic, review APPENDIX
A for preparatory material.

HAASE'S DEMISE

Hasse catches a bad disease that has no cure. Knowing that he is dying, he prepares his will. His son, Moe-Haar, is too young to be given responsibilities. Therefore, Hasse calls on his only brother Mead to take care of Moe-Haar. Hasse also pronounces Mead recipient of all his wealth and property. Furthermore, Hasse asks that Mead take good care of the poor people who live with him, especially Beebe and Pascal.

Hasse dies in peace. He is buried. Everyone is sad. Moe-Haar especially feels that he is alone and lost-nobody will ever be able to replace his father. Hasse had always been a great wall for Moe-Haar to lean on. Now that great wall is gone.

MEAD'S TAKEOVER

With Hasse's death, Mead gains control. But Mead is not as kind as Hasse was, and together he and his evil wife hatch a spiteful, wicked plan.

Mead begins by forcing the poor inhabitants of the palace out onto the streets, with nowhere else to go. He also fires Pascal from his job, since Mead does not appreciate knowledge.

But getting rid of Moe-Haar and Beebe is not as easy for Mead. Although Beebe has no power, Moe-Haar is Mead's nephew and Mead must take care of him. Mead realizes the only way to escape his responsibility is to have Moe-Haar killed.

Meanwhile, Beebe senses that all is not well in the palace. She decides she has no choice but to eavesdrop. Creeping down the hall, she overhears Mead and his wife as they plot to have Moe-Haar destroyed.

Alone in the black of the night, Beebe understands that she must save Moe-Haar from danger.

ESCAPING TO THE WOODS

While the palace sleeps, Beebe creeps into Moe-Haar's room to awaken him. Although he is shocked and confused, he doesn't demand an explanation.

Beebe and Moe-Haar move quickly through the palace since most of the guards are asleep. But at the gates of the palace they find more guards, and these are awake. Quickly, Beebe and Moe-Haar escape through an underground passageway that leads to the forest.

When he realizes the following morning that they are missing, Mead is furious. Enraged, he orders that all guards be punished for allowing Beebe and Moe-Haar to escape.

Furthermore, he offers a handsome reward for Beebe and Moe-Haar's capture and return to the palace.

SETTLING DOWN

After they had crept quietly out of the palace, Beebe and Moe had to search for a place where they would be able to settle down without being noticed. Beebe immediately remembers her mother's old hut in the woods, and decides it is where she and Moe will stay.

Beebe knows that Moe needs to pursue his education with Pascal. Therefore, she secretly sends for Pascal to come and teach Moe. Knowledge is the only weapon Moe can use to battle his enemies.

Pascal welcomes the idea of educating Moe, and takes the opportunity to establish a community near Beebe's hut where all of the poor and the needy people Mead threw out will be able to live. Although these people are feeble now, once they unite and get their feet on the ground, they will certainly be a veritable threat to injustice. Pascal thus plays two roles: educator to Moe-Haar, and compassionate leader for these helpless people.

Beebe anticipates that Mead will offer a reward for her and Moe-Haar's capture. Fearful that they will be recognized, she resolves to change their appearances to disguise their identities. She costumes Moe-Haar as a girl, and costumes herself as a gipsy.

Pascal knows that any coup d'état that does not value knowledge, regardless of how strong it is at the beginning, will end up being crushed; therefore, he does not want to waste any energy on fighting back. The evil shall destroy itself one day. Once corruption prevails, everything falls apart. Then will come the right time to attack.

Everybody sets to work, making any effort to build up the new camp community. Nobody remains idle: some cut wood, some build the colony, some cultivate lands, some dig for water, some cook, some watch the young children, some teach, and some keep busy through a variety of tasks.

THE SEARCH BEGINS

As soon as Mead realizes that Beebe and Moe have escaped, he becomes restless and anxious. He knows that his newfound power and prosperity will be threatened sooner or later. Beebe and Moe must be brought back one way or another.

Mead calls on all of his followers to go after Beebe and Moe. The reward for their capture is high and worth the trouble. Mead sends people in all directions: some to the sea, some to the woods, some to the farms, and some to town.

Xeng leads the woods group. He is intent on claiming the reward. He has utterly forgotten all the good deeds Hasse did for him.

Xeng passes by Pascal and his people, and disrupts the tranquility of their camp by overturning any and all places where Beebe or Moe might be hiding. He demands all the young boys and women to form a queue in order to inspect them, and is enraged when he does not find Beebe or Moe. Grudgingly, he leaves the area to look some-where else.

While Xeng and his men search the area, Pascal sends two of his own men to inform Beebe of what is going on.

Upon receiving the message, Beebe and Moe take refuge in the hut's hidden basement.

Xeng reaches the hut and explores it, but moves on after a short time. He searches the woods for days, weeks, and months. Eventually, Xeng gives up on ever finding them, and reluctantly decides to abandon his barren search.

Xeng is not alone. Everyone else who searched found nothing. Mead is not at all happy with the result of the searches, and punishes Xeng and all the other leaders for their failure.

Pascal, Beebe, Moe-Haar, and the other people of the community all work hard to achieve their noble goal. After settling down, the first thing they do is to start a school. Education is what Pascal values above all else—with proper education and knowledge, the impossible can become a reality.

But education requires continuous, dedicated, and serious work. Pascal is continually preaching this fact; yet he makes time for entertainment, too. Along with the newly constructed school, many amusement facilities have been built. Pascal encourages people to go outdoors to release their daily pressure. Moreover, people need to be aware of time and its management. A good balance between work and play is ideal.

Pascal classifies people with different talents to work on their fields and teach others as well. The new colony is full of people with all different talents. But although these people are different in their aptitudes and abilities, they all have two common ideas in mind: to share and be sincere.

Of course, Moe-Haar has received special attention from Pascal and Beebe, but certainly not because he used to be rich; wealth is ultimately meaningless and can be detrimental if possessed by the wrong people. Rather, Moe-Haar receives this attention because he is Hasse's legal heir; therefore, he is the only one who can reclaim his and other people's rights. Moreover, he is receptive, intelligent, and loves to learn. This is of course in addition to his respect for Pascal and his trust in Beebe.

HAVOC OF VILES

Mead's main aim is to seize wealth and power. Therefore, he starts to bribe those people in power in order to accomplish his evil goals. Once vice inducement starts, corruption prevails. Once corruption prevails, havoc rules.

Mead becomes the ultimate indirect ruler-his wishes are blindly satisfied. Of course, the public protests such behavior, and so Mead and his gang must redirect the public's attention. Most of the public is easily deceived.

First, Mead assaults the schooling system. He invades and occupies the only available school in town and turns it into a barn for horses and other domestic animals. Not only that, Mead changes the whole education system from a fruitful enterprise into a vain one.

The hopeless people rent a house to replace the abducted school. Unfortunately, they cannot change the enforced new schooling system. The history has been changed from an objective opinion into a biased trifle that exalts worthless and weightless individuals. The analytical subjects (such as mathematics) have been modified into Byzantines. Decency has transformed to depravity and vice versa.

With time, the public changes from gratified into avaricious. Ethics have no meaning. People want to grow at the expense of others. Cheating dominates. The strong destroy the vulnerable. Corruption becomes the norm. Hence, everyone becomes blind to what in fact happens behind the scenes.

CONSEQUENCES

As time goes by, the inhabitants of Pascal's colony grow stronger and more satisfied; meanwhile, the townspeople become increasingly weak and miserable. Likewise, Moe-Haar grows to be a kind, scholarly, and able-bodied young man, while Joe-Haar remains a spoiled adolescent, cowardly yet malicious and brutal.

Pascal's people are prosperous, benevolent individuals, free to make their own decisions. The townspeople, on the other hand, have lost all dignity. They cower in fear in Mead's presence.

Mead is well aware of the power he holds over the townspeople and does not want to lose this control. Rather than rely on his own guards, he employs foreign mercenaries to protect him. He no longer even trusts his own people!

History has indicated that good and liberal people can live in harmony with others. The people of Sea-Hat are no exception.

Sarah, an inhabitant of Sea-Hat, is a beautiful and wise young lady. She possesses many outstanding attributes that make her exceptional. Every young man in town wishes to marry her. Joe-Haar has already had his eye on her. To him, she is easy to get-her father is one of the toadies of the palace, and thus would never be able to refuse Joe-Haar's wish. If he ever did, he would be doomed. Yet Sarah has no desire to marry Joe-Haar.

Sarah adores nature and outdoor activities that stimulate and recharge her imagination. She often enjoys going to the woods to relax and meditate. One day, Joe-Haar decides to follow her to the woods. While she is meditating, Joe-Haar approaches her. She asks him to leave peacefully, but he refuses. As Joe-Haar moves to block her path out of the forest so that she cannot escape him, a knight on his horse comes storming out of the trees to Sarah's rescue. "This is like a dream," she thinks, as she looks up at the knight. Meanwhile, Joe-Haar, cowardly in nature, runs instantly from the scene.

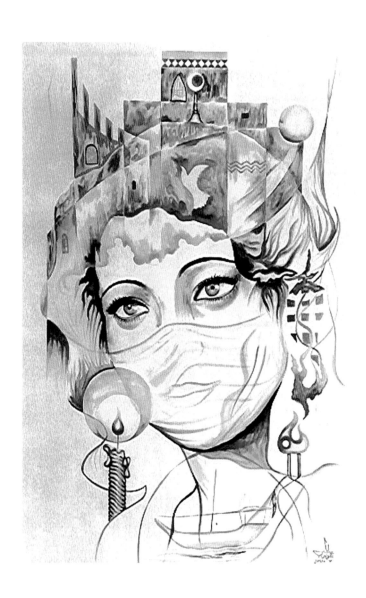

A SPARK OF LOVE

Isolated from others, Moe-Haar has not had the chance to meet many new people. But now, before him, he sees a beautiful girl face to face. His heart starts to palpitate faster than usual. His eyes grow wider. His body sweats. Everything feels like a sudden shock to him.

Sarah, too, is moved by his presence. She has never before seen a man who could stand against Joe-Haar. Moe-Haar's bravery, posture, solemnity, eloquence, dignity, and confidence are not common-this young man deserves respect and admiration. And more than all this, he is the first man ever to capture Sarah's heart.

Moe-Haar does not know how to express his feelings, but his facial expressions are enough. He stands speechless, gazing at Sarah. Sarah understands immediately that he is a true savior.

Sarah asks to know the identity of the courageous knight, but Moe-Haar is well trained and cannot reveal his true self. She senses that he is keeping his identity secret for good reasons, and therefore does not try to force a reply.

In reality, they both become acquainted with each other. Neither of them wants to leave his or her partner.

Sarah wants to have another date with Moe-Haar. She has to tell him about all the misery they face every day. She wants to reveal her discomfort because of Joe-Haar, and the pressure she faces because of her disagreement with the arranged marriage enforced by her father.

Both of them meet many times later until the spark of love welds their souls together. She has become the eye for Moe-Haar as to what happens in town. In his turn, he delivers all the news to Pascal and Beebe. Moe-Haar still keeps the secrets to himself, but not because he does not trust Sarah. He does not mix emotion with rationalism. This is a very important quality of any patriot solider. Moreover, he does not want to hurt Sarah because this knowledge can turn to a peril. What he has in mind is a mission-critical task.

DECLARING MARRIAGE

Joe-Haar is suspicious of Sarah's frequent visits to the woods, yet he is too frightened to go after her. His power is in Sea-Hat-the woods are not his turf.

Instead, he demands that Sarah's father allow Joe-Haar to marry Sarah. But when Sarah refuses, her father is left defenseless-he can neither refuse Joe-Haar's wish nor force his daughter into an undesired marriage. As punishment, Sarah's father is sent to prison. The malevolent Joe-Haar approaches Sarah and offers her a choice: either she marries Joe-Haar, or her father will be hanged.

Although she has no desire to marry Joe-Haar, Sarah cannot let him have her father killed. And so she agrees to the marriage.

Joe-Haar decides to wait a week to declare the marriage. Meanwhile, he confines Sarah to the palace. No visitors are allowed. Alas, she cannot deliver the news to Moe-Haar.

A WORD TO THE WISE IS ENOUGH

Moe-Haar senses Sarah's unusual disappearance. He is not a fool. He approaches Beebe immediately. She can see the love, passion, and yearning on his face. She cannot put him down.

Beebe has trained an orphan bulbul that can fly back and forth and can carry messages. She ties a message on the bulbul's leg saying, "If there is a problem in town, the woods are on fire." The bulbul does not know Sarah. How can it deliver the message to her? But animals can identify people from their smells, not their faces. Beebe asks Moe-Haar if he has any souvenir from Sarah. Fortunately, he does not go anywhere without Sarah's handkerchief with its astonishing aroma. Beebe lets the bulbul sniff the handkerchief and then lets it loose.

Both Beebe and Moe-Haar wait anxiously for the result.

The bulbul flies away toward the town. Luckily, the town is not very big. After roaming around, it finally finds Sarah. It lands on her shoulder and starts to untie the message. Well, Sarah is prudent and she knows what the bulbul is trying to convey to her. She reads the message and understands its connotation. Sarah always carries a pen with her; therefore, she will not find any difficulty responding, saying, "The hideous crow is consuming the captive dove."

The bulbul flies back to Moe Haar with the message, which Moe-Haar has no difficulty understanding.

THE HOARD

Moe-Haar has no patience. Joe-Haar has stolen the affluence, which can be recovered; but people are more precious and they cannot be replaced. Therefore, Moe-Haar is forced to retort. Losing his parents is enough. Moe-Haar cannot afford to lose more valued people.

Moe-Haar decides to assail the gang in town. Beebe wants to cool him down. Beebe proposes a different plan. She likes to resolve the problem more peacefully. She wants to avoid harassing the innocents. Usually, in wars, many civilians get victimized.

Beebe advises Moe-Haar to unlock the mystery that has not yet been deciphered. He possesses all the criteria needed for such task, which is to get the two magical wands from a buried treasure.

Beebe takes Moe-Haar to the treasure site that most people do not know about. Beebe instructs him to what to do. She explains every final detail. No mistakes are allowed. Any mistake leads to death.

Beebe tells him to enter the cave slowly, yet with dignity. His heart should be fearless. His soul should be greedless. After passing the cave, he will see a room; he needs to knock on its door thrice before going in. Inside the room, there is a lioness, which could be either dangerous or peaceful: this of course depends on the intruder's intentions. In order to pass the lioness and get into the second passage, Moe-Haar needs to rub her neck until she relocates herself.

The second passage leads to another room that possesses a couple of tigers that are identical and none can tell them apart. But one of them can only state the truth and the other can only mislead. Each of them is protecting a passenger-bridge. One bridge leads to the treasure room and the other leads to perdition. Moe is allowed one question only, no second; otherwise, the tigers eat him.

If Moe-Haar succeeds to pass the correct bridge, he will get into the King's room that is protected by a lion. The lion sits atop an ancient treasure box. Moe-Haar needs to coax the lion to loosen guarding the coffer, but how? Beebe does not know the answer. Moe needs to open the coffer to get the two magical wands.

THE CRITICAL MISSION

Moe-Haar is ready to go into the cave. Before he leaves, Beebe prays and adorns his neck with a periapt. As he gets into the mouth of the cave, she sings a mantra to protect him.

Without fear, Moe-Haar enters the cave. He sees a long and desolate passageway ahead. However, this cannot trigger a forlorn hope inside him. He walks forward with solely one thing in mind: to attain possession of the magical wands.

He reaches the first room. He bravely and politely knocks three times at the door. The door abruptly opens with a squeaking noise that would frighten anyone-but not Moe-Haar. He confidently enters through the door. To his surprise, he sees walls studded with gold and diamonds. What he sees can trick others, but not him. Greed does not exist in his agenda.

In the dark, ephemerally, Moe-Haar sees two glazing spots from a distance. As he gets closer, he realizes that those are the lioness's eyes. He approaches the lioness and gently pats her neck. After a while, she reacts to his placid hand. Dutifully, she yields to allow him to pass.

Now, Moe-Haar is walking toward the second room and thinking how to use his only question astutely. It did not take him long to face the tigers. Although the room is full of ores and other precious stones, Moe-Haar does not care, and probably does not realize their existence. He looks up at the tigers' huge faces not knowing how to communicate with them nor what to ask.

Suddenly, he recalls Pascal's teaching of logic. That can help him resolve the mystery! How can Moe-Haar ask only one question to lead him to the right path? Logic has to be used; otherwise, there is no escape. Consult with APPENDIX B to see how Moe-Haar uses logic to resolve his problem.

Now, can you help Moe-Haar ask his question? Well, he is acute, isn't he? Therefore, he should come up with a very good question. Most probably, he already drew it from the table.

Moe-Haar is approaching one of the tigers and asking it: "If I asked your mate about the right path, which one would it say?" The tiger reverses its seating pointing to the door it is guarding. Moe-Haar immediately knows that the other conduit is the safe path.

If we analyze Moe-Haar's logic, we can depict that he does not need to know who tells the truth. If he asked

the truthful tiger, it would say the truth about the other tiger, which does not tell the truth, i.e. it would point to the wrong path. Therefore, Moe-Haar should take the other suggested path. Now, if he asked the lying tiger, it would not say the truth about the truthful tiger. It would point to the one the truthful tiger would not suggest.

Therefore, Moe-Haar is safe in both cases by knowing 100% that the returned answer would always be false. Thanks to logic: it is simple, yet powerful.

Now, Moe-Haar is confidently walking through the safe route to the treasure room. The closer he gets to the room, the gloomier the passageway becomes and the faster his heart beats. He enters the room and sees a giant lion above the treasure box. Since he is thinking about how to approach the lion, Moe-Haar walks around the room. The lion's eyes follow him wherever he goes.

With time, Moe-Haar becomes more comfortable with the situation and gets closer to the lion. While he walks towards the lion, Moe-Haar remembers that he patted the lioness earlier; therefore, her odor should be fresh on his hands. For that reason, he moves toward the lion more assertively and starts to rub its nose. Suddenly, the giant cat stands up and gyrates around Moe-Haar while rubbing its body against him like a small kitten.

Now Moe-Haar can take the magical wands. He opens the chest and sees two small wands made of genuine ivory. He places them in his pocket, closes the coffer, and heads back to Beebe.

MISFORTUNES NEVER COME SINGLY

While Beebe is waiting for Moe-Haar, Joe-Haar goes hunting with his train. Unfortunately, he happens to find where Beebe is. He starts interrogating her immediately. This is not a normal place for people to come to, especially old ladies. She becomes nervous because she is afraid that the mean Joe-Haar discloses the great secret. Therefore, she does not welcome him and tries to keep him away.

Although Joe-Haar is not very smart, his evil spirit makes him suspect a conspiracy. He starts harassing poor Beebe and enjoys torturing her. As she is standing, he tries to knock her with his horse. He is skilled at tormenting people! She stands bravely against his brutality, but finally collapses and falls down.

Nonetheless, he does not leave her alone. He starts lashing her haphazardly with his whip. Being an old lady, she cannot long tolerate such an affliction.

By the time Moe-Haar gets out of the cave, he sees the brutality of Joe-Haar to Beebe. He rushes immediately to the scene, but Joe-Haar escapes.

By the time Moe-Haar arrives, Beebe can barely speak. He wants to chase after Joe-Haar, but she stops him because she wants to tell him something before she passes away.

Beebe wants to reveal the secret of the wands. These wands are magical, and only good people can use them. They can never be abused, but they can batter abusers. Therefore, one should use them wisely.

The way these wands operate is easy. One needs only to tap them against each other three times. After the first time, the spirits of the big cats hover around their master. After the second time, their ghosts accompany their master. And after the third time, the cats themselves escort their master. Once they are physically present, their master can command anything of them.

As soon as the last words have left her mouth, Beebe passes away. Moe-Haar drops to his knees, wailing over her body. He does not realize that Joe-Haar and his gang have begun to surround him. Joe-Haar accuses Moe-Haar of killing Beebe and commands that his mercenaries arrest him. Moe-Haar is charged with Beebe's murder and detained and taken to jail.

Moe-Haar is stunned speechless. He is locked inside a carthorse and taken back to Sea-Hat. Yet he thinks of nothing else than having lost Beebe.

As the cart reaches the city, Moe-Haar starts hearing the shindy of people in town. He remembers the two magical wands. The time has come to use them, but his hands are tied behind his back. He tries to twist his torso so that he can reach the wands, but only manages to grab one-he drops the second one, which starts rolling out of the cart.

Suddenly, the cart stops in front of the jail downtown. Moe-Haar feels a little relief to know that the wand is not far.

Joe-Haar orders that the Sheriff hang Moe-Haar the next day while Joe-Haar celebrates his wedding to Sarah. The Sheriff can say nothing but "Yes, sir." Moe-Haar says "What. When was the trial and who was the judge?" "Judge and trial!" both the Sheriff and Joe-Haar hoot, "We have no need of those!"

GOD DISPOSES, MAN PROPOSES

Although he is jailed, Moe-Haar refuses to give up. He still has hope that he will overcome his circumstances.

Moe-Haar starts poking through the window whose bottom-edge is level with the ground. After a while, he spots the missing wand some distance away. "How can I reach it?" Moe-Haar contemplates.

Moe-Haar notices some children playing around the corner. He must get their attention. He starts throwing small stones in their direction. The children turn and see him, but they are hostile. They begin picking up random objects from the ground and throwing them at him. One of them picks up the wand, which hits the outside wall of the jail and bounces back two meters (around 6.5 feet) away. This is what Moe-Haar is waiting for.

But the wand is still too far for Moe-Haar to reach-he needs something to reach it. He calls to the jail guard and asks to be brought the long stick used to chastise outlaws. "Why?" the guard asks. "I usually like to punish myself whenever I sin," Moe-Haar replies. "This is good thinking son," the guard says, and fetches the stick and passes it to Moe-Haar.

Moe-Haar uses the stick to try to pull the wand closer to his window. Despite the slow progress, he does not give up. But suddenly, as he is pulling the wand closer, a carthorse passes by, running over the stick and breaking it. Magically, the wand disappears altogether.

Heart-broken, Moe-Haar returns half of the stick to the jailer, who thinks that breaking the stick shows that Moe-Haar did a good job of punishing himself.

Moe-Haar cannot sleep. He is waiting and thinking about the unfair tribunal he has had. Yet he still believes that he is going to thwart the conspiracy. He stays up until dawn.

He hears a cart approach the jail, stopping at the gate. He hears the sound of muffled voices but he cannot make out what's being said. After a short while, two guards come in to Moe-Haar's cell and escort him out to the cart, which is heading to decapitation court.

Moe's hands are tied behind him. He only has one part of the wand. He is inside a tumbrel, waiting for the death penalty. His brain is winding very fast.

Suddenly Moe-Haar hears some object thumping the left side of the cart, behind his back. He stops all of his other thoughts and heeds to the sound and its source. As he looks back, he sees the magical wand entangled within the rim of the wheel.

He would achieve his goal if he could get the two wands struck against each other. At first, it may sound easy to attain; but with tied hands, it is difficult to accomplish the required accuracy, especially when playing against time. Nonetheless, this is the only chance Moe-Haar has.

Moe-Haar carefully reaches into his pocket and firmly grips the wand. Without losing it, he needs to pass it through the hole to align it with the revolving wand. Before starting, Moe-Haar rehearses this task in his mind. He takes a deep breath, steadily holds the wand, and passes it through the hole.

He misses the first revolution, but he catches the second. Now, he feels the spirits of the cats. As the cart moves, he tries to get the next hit. Eventually he gets the second strike. Now, he sees the ghosts of the cats. He needs only one more smack and the game is over to his advantage. Let's hope it will be successful!

Generally, all's well that ends well. But sometimes, the wind does not blow in the direction people want. As Moe-Haar is trying for a third hit, the cart suddenly stops. What! The cart reaches its destination before Moe-Haar's luck can favor him.

The only choice left for him is to throw his wand haphazardly, hoping it will collide with the second one. And so he does this, but ………… it does not hit the other wand.

Providentially, a snake turns up in front of the horses, which forces them to retreat. While they do, the two wands collide.

EVERYTHING COMES TO HIM WHO WAITS

The guards come to open the door of the cart. Unexpectedly, the big cats jump one after another, except the lion. The crowd becomes terrified. Riding the lion's back, Moe-Haar exits the cart. All the guards and mercenaries flee.

While still riding the lion, Moe-Haar leads the flock to the wedding location. Stupefied, everyone stares at this inimitable incident. Moe-Haar reaches the wedding and heralds, "the ebb of iniquity has come."

Joe-Haar asks his bodyguards to prevent Moe-Haar from reaching the groom, but who could? Moe-Haar is moving forward until he reaches the quivering Joe-Haar. "Why don't you arrest him," Joe-Haar yells. "Why don't you try it," Moe-Haar replies.

Moe stands up and states that Joe-Haar is the murderer of Beebe. "He is bluffing. Don't believe him," Joe-Haar says. "I'm not going to judge you. I'll let the two tigers do it in front of the public. They love to eat the flesh of liars," Moe-Haar retorts.

It is true that those two tigers eat liars. They cannot tolerate lying whatsoever. Therefore, as soon as Joe-Haar starts to lie to the public, the tigers furiously roar and show their fangs.

53

Joe-Haar realizes that he cannot lie anymore; otherwise, he would have to face stern consequences. Therefore, he confesses to killing Beebe. However, he claims that he did not intend to do that initially.

Hearing the source of the noise, Mead Haar (Joe's father) hurries up to the show. He cannot recognize Moe-Haar though the opposite is not true. Moe-Haar asks him about his wealth and influence. As soon as Mead starts to flaunt, the two tigers roar. He is so shocked he loses consciousness.

The public is already fed up with Joe and Mead Haar and the corruption they have brought to the peaceful town. The people could not protest in the past; now it is their chance to blow away the dark clouds.

While these activities take place, Moe's army arrives. They are those trained by Pascal and those who have respected and admired Moe-Haar. He is very pleased to see them arrive at the right time. He wonders why they have come. They told him they came to free and fight for him. After all, they cannot let anything bad happen to their estimable leader.

Nothing else is left except declaring a new era under a revised constitution and proper people to lead the nation. The whole population vote for this. Nobody else is left to protect Joe and Mead nor the corrupted politicians. All the mercenaries have escaped. Joe Haar, his father, and other tarnished people are being sent to jail for a fair trial once everything has settled down.

THERE IS A TIME FOR ALL THINGS

After having everything grasped in hand, Moe-Haar announces a democratic republic that is run by the people. No room is left for corruption. Honest auditors are now all over the place. People who have been trained by Pascal are leading the ship safely toward shore.

Moe-Haar recovers his wealth and marries Sarah, who-willingly and happily accepts this marriage. On the day of his wedding, a parade is formed to go around town. The parade passes the jail where Joe-Haar resides. He sees the happiness of the people and Sarah; meanwhile, his sorrows are entertaining him.

After an honest election, Moe-Haar is elected to be the president for four years. Under his era, the living standard dramatically improves, education system advances, and happiness prevails.

Moe-Haar dedicates his cats to the town. He lends the two tigers to the main court; meanwhile, keeps the two lions protect the town's front. He also donates great deal of his wealth for welfare and to help bring up the town and its people.

Let us all hope the best for this peaceful town and try to apply some of the good things we have learned and avoid evil and bad issues. Let us all equip ourselves with proper knowledge and education, in addition to good manners and sharing attitudes.

EXERCISES

Q1: Please, match synonyms:

Word	Synonym	Select From
Bitter		Flatterer
Decorate		Acrimonious
Fluency		Abjure
Panacea		Evil
Renounce		Abet
Serendipitous		Stiff
Stern		Weak
Sycophant		Adorn
Tyrant		Dictator
Urge		Eloquence
Vile		Unexpected
Vulnerable		Universal remedy

Q2: Use words from Q1 to complete the following sentences:

1. Isaac Newton discovered gravity _____ly.

2. Can I get a _____ to cure all diseases?

3. This little animal is _____ for predators.

4. We need to _____ our living room with some art.

5. All scholars _____ people to be good to each other.

6. The public does not welcome _____ leaders.

7. Outlaws face _____ consequences.

8. Lucifer is the master of _____.

9. I cannot be a _____ for the big bully.

10. Good vocabulary increases _____.

Q3: Do you think it is wise to abuse power or knowledge?

Q4: What makes Moe-Haar a noble person?

Q5: What are the consequences facing Joe-Haar?

Q6: Why do you think that corruption is bad for the country?

Q7: If you had a friend that did a bad thing, would you cover up for him? Why?

Q8: Do you think lying or covering guilty people will help them?

Q9: Do you agree with the following: if lying is safe, truth is safer.

Q10: I can accept punishment if I sin. What about you?

Q11: If you were a leader, would you apply the law to everyone, including yourself and your loved ones? Why?

Q12: Can you live in an environment where everyone hates you? How can avoid being hated?

Q13: Detergents may help clean clothes. How can we clean human spirits?

Q14: Do you think that love is important? Explain and give an example.

Q15: If you had enough food and your neighbor were hungry, what would you do?

Q16: If you were a rich farmer, would you throw extra crops to the fishes (in the ocean) in order to maintain good prices, or would you rather distribute them to needy people?

Q17: Is it wise to be always emotional? Or you think we need to be only rational? Or maybe we need to mix the two? Why?

APPENDIX A

PREPARATORY MATERIAL

Consider the following table:

Person	True statement	False statement
Someone	The fire is hot	The fire is cold.
Student	2 + 2 = 4.	2 + 2 = 5.
Logical representation	T	F

Table 1

As can be seen, the previous statements can be either true or false. <u>There is no third state.</u> Thus, the binary logic can only have two states: True[3] and False[4].

Logical States
T
F

Table 2

---

[3]For short, it will be represented as T.

[4]For short, it will be represented as F.

What if people want to negate a statement (whether true or false)? For instance, can someone negate the previous statement (i.e. "The fire is hot.")?

Well, negating this statement is not difficult. One can say, "The fire is NOT hot." But then the generated statement is false. This is not surprising since negating anything true produces something that is not true, or false. After all, the fire can never be anything else but hot. Now take a look at the following table:

State A	Negation of A	A	Ã
T	F	The fire is hot.	The fire is not hot.
F	T	The fire is cold.	The fire is not cold.

Table 3

In the table above, the logical state is represented as the letter A. It is already known that any logical state can only take two values: either true (T) or false (F). Negating these two states will result in their opposites (i.e. F and T), respectively. An example of two statements is given: the first one is true and the second one is false. The statements are then negated in order to prove their negation results. The original statements are referred to by the letter A; meanwhile, their negation statements are referred to by Ã, which, in the language of logic, always means the negation of A. These symbolic representations are given in order to eliminate too much writing, because prolix writing can result into an unwieldy table!

Dealing only with the true and false states for a single predicate may not make much sense. Therefore, mathematicians join the results of these predicates with different operators, such as AND, OR, and some others.

Here, we will address only the AND operator. Joining two predicates with AND can generate the following four states:

AND	T	F
T	T	F
F	F	F

Table 4: The truth table of the AND operator.

We know that having any predicate can only result in either T or F, i.e. any given statement can be either true (such as "the fire is hot"), or false (such as "the fire is cold").

For example, let us consider the following two statements and try to join their states:

True	False
The fire is hot.	The fire is cold.
The water is wet.	The water is dry.

Table 5

AND	The water is wet	The water is dry
The fire is hot	True	False
The fire is cold	False	False

Table 6

The above table produces the following for statements:

1. The fire is hot and the water is wet.

2. The fire is hot and the water is dry.

3. The fire is cold and the water is wet.

4. The ~~water~~ fire is cold and the water is dry.

Now use your own judgment to see which of the above statements makes sense. Got it? Right, only No. 1 makes sense—none of the other three statements do. Therefore, using the AND operator, the resulting predicate can be true only when both combined predicates are already true. This is why mathematicians came up with the truth table (look back to review the truth table of the AND operator shown earlier).

If you are not sure about your understanding of logic, ask one of your parents (or any other adult) to explain it to you. Although it is not necessary to understand this material (i.e. logic) to proceed with the story, awareness is recommended.

APPENDIX B

Moe-Haar draws the following table in his mind:

Row	T1	T2	T1∧T2	~(T1∧T2)
1	T	T	T	F
2	T	F	F	T
3	F	T	F	T
4	F	F	F	T

Table 7

Moe-Haar, now, is using some strange symbols used with logical operators. They are not strange if people can tell what they mean. They are actually easy to know:

Symbol	Meaning
T1	The answer of the first tiger.
T2	The answer of the second tiger.
T1∧T2	Combining the answers of the first tiger and second one using the AND operator.
~(T1∧T2)	Negating the result of T1∧T2.
∧	This symbol used in logic to mean the AND operator.
~	This symbol, known as a tilde, is used to negate the result of something, e.g. ~A = NOT A.
( )	Parentheses are used to mean first evaluate what is inside before applying any other external operator. The case, ~(T1∧T2), means first evaluate what is inside the parentheses, and then negate its value.

Table 8

Note, in Table 7, rows 1 and 4 are not of interest. Only rows 2 and 3 are of concern because in row 2 the first tiger is telling the truth while the second is not. The third row is the opposite of row 2. This is the case Moe-Haar is facing. He does not know which one is truthful, but he knows one thing: if he could combine both of their answers into one, the result would always be false. Negating the resultant leads him to the answer of interest.